For Aja...Our Hero.

You are more than just Trey Amani's little sister, you are
a strong, independent, and loving young lady. We love you
a billion, trillion, gazillion times more!

Mommy and Daddy

www.mascotbooks.com

The Sensationally Super Sandy

For more information, please contact:
Mascot Books
620 Herndon Parkway, Suite 320
Herndon, VA 20170
info@mascotbooks.com

Library of Congress Control Number: 2020902786

CPSIA Code: PRT0520A
ISBN-13: 978-1-64543-439-9

Printed in the United States

THE SENSATIONALLY SUPER SANDY

Jamiyl Samuels &
Tracy-Ann Samuels

Illustrated by iNDOS Studios

Sandy Taylor was a
wonderful little girl.

She was a free spirit who liked to
draw and swim, but she especially
loved dancing.

At school, Sandy had lots of friends to talk to, but at home she had no one to play with. She played school with her dolls, pretending to be a teacher, but they didn't talk back when she called on them or asked them questions.

She tried to get her older brother, Amani, to play with her, but he wouldn't talk, either! Whenever she tried to talk to him, he just smiled back at her or laughed.

"Stop laughing at me!" Sandy yelled, but Amani just laughed harder in response.

Sandy was so upset; she ran off to tell her Mommy and Daddy.

"What's wrong, Sandy?" Daddy asked as she ran into the room.

"Amani's making fun of me," she whined. "I tried to get him to play school with me, but he keeps laughing!"

Mommy held Sandy's hands and drew her close. "Amani is not laughing at you," Mommy explained. "He just has a hard time putting words together."

"But he's older than me,"
Sandy snapped back.

"Amani is special,"
Daddy explained.

"I'm special, too!"
Sandy yelled.

"Of course you are, sweetheart," Mommy said.
"Amani just has some challenges."

"What kind of challenges?" Sandy asked.

"Have you ever noticed how when Amani walks around, he flaps his hands close to his face?" Mommy asked.

"Or how when he hears loud noises, he runs out of the room covering his ears?" Daddy continued.

"There are times when he can't sit still—" Mommy started.

"That's all the time," Sandy interrupted. "It's so annoying!"

"Well, he can't help it," Mommy said. "Your brother has Autism."

"What's Autism?" Sandy asked.

"It's a disorder that makes it hard for Amani to speak or interact socially with other kids. Imagine not being able to talk to your friends because you don't know what to say," Mommy explained.

"So, he doesn't know what to say to me?" Sandy asked.

"That's right," Mommy said. "So, when he smiles at you, that's his way of communicating."

"You know how at school it's easy for you to make friends and talk to other kids?" Daddy asked.

Sandy nodded.

"Amani doesn't know how to do that. He needs to be taught."

"How did that happen to him?"

Mommy and Daddy looked at each other.

"We're not quite sure," Mommy said. "But he's in a good school that will give him the help he needs to work on his speech."

"There's a girl in my class named Annabelle who does the same things that Amani does," Sandy said.

"She does?" Mommy asked.

"Yes. She likes to sit under the table," Sandy offered, "and she's always moving back and forth."

"And what do you think about that?" Daddy asked.

"I think it's funny," Sandy laughed.

"Sandy, that's not nice,"
Mommy warned.

Sandy stopped laughing. "Maybe she can't stop herself
from moving back and forth," Mommy said. "What else does
Annabelle do?"

"She doesn't talk. She just stares at me."

"Do you talk to her?" Daddy asked.

"Yeah!" Sandy said. "I tell her to 'Stop looking at me!' and 'Get away from me!'"

"How do you think that makes her feel when you talk to her like that?" Mommy asked.

Daddy leaned in closer to Sandy. "Imagine how you'd feel if other kids bullied you because they thought you couldn't fight back."

"That's not bullying! I'm not a bully! You're just taking her side because she's like Amani and you love him more than me!" Sandy yelled as she ran out of the room.

"Can I come in?" Daddy asked peeking his head in Sandy's room.

Sandy nodded.

"What does the 'S' stand for?" he asked as he sat next to her.

"I'm making a costume," Sandy grumbled. "Tomorrow is Superhero Day at school. I'm going to be a superhero...Super Sandy!"

"That's awesome," Daddy said.

"Not awesome," Sandy corrected. "Sensational!"

Daddy was impressed. "Sensational? That's a big word, Princess."

"It's better than awesome!" Sandy proclaimed.

Daddy took a deep breath. "Sandy, you said Mommy and I love Amani more than you. What makes you think that?"

Sandy looked up at Daddy with narrow eyes. "Why should I tell you?" she said. "You don't care anyway."

"That's not true, Sandy. Mommy and I love you very much." Daddy reached down, picked Sandy up, and twirled her around. "You're our **BEAUTIFUL, SPECTACULAR, SENSATIONAL** little girl. There is no one else like you!" he said as he put Sandy down.

"But all you talk about is Amani all the time! He gets extra attention at school and at bedtime. I barely get any time with you at all," Sandy pouted.

"We're sorry that we made you feel you're not as special to us as Amani," Daddy said. "A person with Autism requires a lot of attention. Not just from Mommy and Daddy, but from doctors, teachers, therapists, and psychologists."

"All those people?" Sandy wondered.

"Yes," Daddy said. "We all want to make sure Amani is able to have lot of friends and talk as much as you do."

Sandy smiled. "I don't talk that much."

"But you have a lot of friends at school, and people to talk to. Do Amani or Anabelle have lots of friends or people to talk with at school?"

Sandy thought for a moment before shaking her head, "No. They usually sit by themselves."

"Do you think a superhero like Sensational Super Sandy would exclude kids like Amani and Annabelle who were a bit different, or do you think she would include them and try to be their friend?" Daddy asked.

"Superheroes protect and include everyone! Tomorrow I'm going to be the most **SENSATIONAL** superhero and be kind to everyone!"

Daddy was more determined than ever. "Then we better get to work! We are going to make such a Sensational costume for you that no one will be able to ignore **SUPER SANDY!**"

"SENSATIONAL SUPER SANDY!"
Sandy shouted.

The next day, Sandy was the star of Superhero Day! All her friends wanted her attention, but she noticed that Annabelle was huddled under a table covering her ears while two older girls, Maribel and Natalie, were standing over her yelling.

"Say something!" yelled Natalie.

"What are you, dumb?" yelled Maribel.

"This looks like a job for the Sensational Super Sandy!" she shouted, running over to help Annabelle.

"What are you doing to Annabelle?" she yelled at the girls.

Both Maribel and Natalie gave Sandy a nasty look. "Mind your own business before we come after you!" barked Maribel.

"You are just a couple of mean girls who can't do anything but say nasty things to people." Sandy exclaimed. "Leave Annabelle alone!"

"What're you gonna do if we don't?" Maribel mocked.

"I'm going to tell the teacher!" Sandy answered.

By now, Sandy had the attention of all the girls and boys in her class. Maribel and Natalie were embarrassed by all the eyes on them. They were so scared of the thought of Sandy telling on them that they turned and walked away.

When Maribel and Natalie were gone, Sandy went and sat on the floor next to Annabelle.

"Hi, Annabelle," Sandy said with a smile. "Are you alright?" Annabelle took her hands away from her ears and smiled at Sandy.

Sandy's other friends came over to the table and sat on the floor with Annabelle.

"What's wrong with her?" one of the girls asked.

"My brother Amani does the same things at home," Sandy explained. "My Daddy says he has Autism."

The other kids looked confused. Sandy reached her hand out to Annabelle.

"Even though Annabelle doesn't talk much, she is still a good person," Sandy explained. "We have to be nice to her."

Annabelle looked at Sandy's hand, then at her face, and started clapping.

"Why is she doing that?" another little girl asked.

"It's all right," Sandy urged. "Her smiling and clapping her hands is how she speaks to us," she told the other kids. "My brother flaps his hands or laughs."

Annabelle continued clapping and smiling at Sandy.

"Aww, you're welcome," Sandy said, smiling and clapping back. The other kids smiled and started clapping too.

Sandy couldn't wait to go home and tell Mommy, Daddy, and Amani how SENSATIONALLY SUPER her day had been.

JAMIYL SAMUELS is the founder of W.R.E.a.C Havoc Enterprises, a company that fosters growth, creativity, and education through informed written content, film, and recorded music. He began his college career as a Theater major at Morgan State University in 1996, but ultimately graduated with a Bachelor's degree in English and a Master's degree in Media Arts with a concentration in screenwriting from Long Island University in Brooklyn, New York. His ultimate goal is to expand the W.R.E.a.C Havoc brand worldwide. He is currently working on various projects related to *The Amazingly Awesome Amani* series and other works based on the importance of Fatherhood in communities of color.

TRACY-ANN SAMUELS is the co-owner and chief operating officer of W.R.E.a.C Havoc Enterprises. She serves as an ambassador for Autism Speaks. She earned her Bachelor's degree in Psychology from Rutgers University and her Master's degree in Social Work from New York University. She has nineteen years of experience in the Social Services field. As a Senior Advisor at New York City Children's Services, she works with children who are Developmentally Delayed, Seriously Emotionally Disturbed, and Medically Fragile.

Her ultimate goal is to assist at-risk children and their families, counsel couples through relationship and/or marital issues, and make an impact in the community by educating parents about the resources available for children and adults with special needs.

The couple resides in New York with their two children.

To the siblings of special needs children. Know that you are loved just as much as your brother or sister. Your love, patience, and protection goes a long way to forming an unforgettable bond.

We would like to acknowledge parents of special needs children everywhere. Continue to advocate for your son or daughter while navigating the sensitive balance of sharing the love to your other kids. You are amazing, they are awesome, together you are SENSATIONAL!